Jonathan Jackson, His Wife, And Many Members Of His Family: Notes And Reminiscences

James Jackson

In the interest of creating a more extensive selection of rare historical book reprints, we have chosen to reproduce this title even though it may possibly have occasional imperfections such as missing and blurred pages, missing text, poor pictures, markings, dark backgrounds and other reproduction issues beyond our control. Because this work is culturally important, we have made it available as a part of our commitment to protecting, preserving and promoting the world's literature. Thank you for your understanding.

Hon. Jonathan Jackson, his Wife, and many Members of his Family.

NOTES AND REMINISCENCES,

PRINTED FOR HIS DESCENDANTS.

Not Published, nor designed for Publication in any manner.

WRITTEN BY HIS SON,

JAMES JACKSON, M. D.

JANUARY, 1866.

BOSTON:
ALFRED MUDGE & SON, PRINTERS, 34 SCHOOL STREET.
1866.

GENERAL REMARKS.

It is my design in the following pages to give some reminiscences of my late father, the Hon. Jonathan Jackson. These pages are not designed for publication. They are printed with a hope that they will afford some gratification to the descendants and friends of my father.

As I shall have occasion to state in what follows, my father passed what might be considered as the most important years of his life in the beautiful town, now the city, of Newburyport, although he was born and died in Boston. It is nearly sixty years since his decease. What follows might as well have been prepared at any time since that event, as now. If it had been done previously to the departure of my elder brother Charles, or my younger brother Patrick, the following memoir would no doubt have been in every way more perfect and, to me, more satisfactory. A few words will explain why my mind has been especially engaged of late, on a subject always interesting to me.

Some years since a library was established in Newburyport for the benefit of its inhabitants. It has, as I understand, been a growing institution, and a very valuable collection of books has already been made there. Within a year past, an old and ample and valuable house has been purchased for this library, and in this the people of Newburyport have desired to place testimonials in honor of their predecessors.

One of the oldest of the sons of this city now living, and who took an important part in establishing the library, though no longer residing among those sons, continues to the present day to feel a warm interest in the affairs of his native town, and to prompt all who are in any way connected with Newburyport to supply materials, however humble, for the purpose described. The photographs, and other pictures of the better known inhabitants of that city, such as could conveniently be procured, and likewise copies of the published works of those connected with the same city, have already been furnished to an amount of some value. Prompted by my friend, Colonel SWETT, the public-spirited gentleman above referred to, I began a few months since to furnish for the library some photographs, and on the back of each of them some brief memoranda in respect to them.

At a later period I procured photographs of my father and of my mother. When I had done this I designed to send copies to the library similar to those which I had supplied in other cases.

I then began to prepare similar notes for the photographs of my parents, but here I found it impossible to place them within the limits afforded on the back of my father's photograph.*

My own descendants are not few at this moment, and I feel that I have not much time now remaining to leave some account of one whom I venerated

---

* The portrait I have mentioned is a photograph taken by J. A. Whipple of Boston, in this month,—November, 1865,—from a painting by the distinguished Copley, in London, in the year 1784. To the very great accuracy of this likeness, I, who am now the only surviving child of Jonathan Jackson, can bear testimony. It was in May, 1785, that this picture was brought home from London, and I well remember that I very often sat so as to see and examine my father's face and figure, the expression of his countenance, and the dress which he continued to wear for some years after the portrait was finished. This was a coat of a deep blue color, with gilt buttons, the waistcoat being to my boyish eyes very handsome, with broad stripes. His whole dress was such as became the fashion of the times, a point as to which he was never negligent. He regarded Boston as his home, and lived there until he left college, but spoke to me often of long visits, during his boyhood and afterwards, to the residence of his uncle Josiah Quincy, Esq., at Braintree. He looked to this uncle as his best friend and counsellor, and from him he always sought and obtained sound advice. To the hospitable house of this uncle, that building now standing in the town of Quincy, and still most honorably known in every respect, my father always looked back with the strongest associations of love and gratitude.

most highly, and whose memory all of his descendants of sufficient age have been constantly learning to love and cherish.

Let me now proceed more formally to the details of my father's life, which were in fact already prepared before these prefatory remarks were written.

JONATHAN JACKSON

was born in Boston in June, 1743. His father was named Edward, and was a merchant. His mother was Dorothy Quincy, of Braintree, in the part of the town now called Quincy. Jonathan derived his name from his grandfather, who was from the Jacksons of Newton, Middlesex County.

Edward Jackson left only one son and one daughter; they survived their parents by many years. Their son entered the College at Cambridge when about fifteen years of age, and passed through his four years, as I believe, without reproach, though without special honors. He certainly did not make any pretensions to great learning, but was fond of reading. He had a valuable library, and I have reason to believe that he was much interested in history and in works of taste.

He was graduated in 1761.

When he left college, he engaged in preparing himself for a mercantile life, and for this purpose took up his residence in Newburyport, where he entered the store of Patrick Tracy, Esq., of whom I shall soon have something more to say. Mr. Jackson was probably influenced in his choice of this pleasant town, by a very close friendship which began in college, and bore a character which seems to have been almost romantic. It was certainly very strong, and continued to be so, as long as they lived. The friend to whom I have referred was Mr. John Lowell, son of the Rev. John Lowell, a congregational clergyman in Newburyport.

I once saw a few letters which had passed between them, written under fancy names, when they were very young, full of tender, warm and romantic feelings. They were not tame certainly in their style of conversation. They discussed all points in strong and decided language. "The differences among men are not very great,"—Lowell would say,—"men are influenced and moulded by external, or accidental circumstances."

"No," Jackson would maintain, "the peculiarity in each case is the result of an original bent or native tendency."

They often differed thus in opinion without any breach in love and good will. Mr. Lowell was the stronger in intellectual powers, in the powers of imagination and in gifts of expression, which were shown in his eloquence at the bar, and in the social circle. He has scarcely left a descendant in either sex, not distinguished, as he was, for this talent.

Mr. Jackson cultivated good taste and good sense, and held to his convictions in spite of the logic of his more learned friend.

The two were not of the same class in college; Mr. Lowell preceded Mr. Jackson by one year.

These two young men lived together, independently, as bachelors. Mr. Lowell engaged in the practice of law, while his friend engaged in commerce and mercantile business. In the arrangement which they made, they both believed that they should continue bachelors permanently. I will not say that this was a boyish decision, but it was an unwise one. It may be added here, that they were both married early in life; and that, ultimately, Mr. Jackson was married twice and Mr. Lowell three times. Both, I believe, were made happy by each alliance.

Mr. J.'s first matrimonial connection was with Miss Barnard, daughter of the Rev. Mr. Barnard, of Salem. Her life was very short, and probably terminated by pulmonary consumption. After a period, not very long, he contracted a second marriage. This was with Miss Hannah Tracy, the only daughter of Capt. Patrick Tracy, already mentioned, under whose guidance Mr. J. had pursued his mercantile education. Their marriage took place in the spring of 1772. She had then very lately arrived at the age of eighteen, and he had nearly reached that of twenty-nine years. It may be added here that Miss Gookin of Hampton, New Hampshire, was Capt. Tracy's second wife, and became the mother of all his children.

About the time of Mr. Jackson's second marriage he built a house in Newburyport, where he then hoped to spend his life. His friend, Mr. Lowell, erected next to it a house very similar to Mr. Jackson's. These were both wooden houses, large in size, and handsome for their day. These friends both supposed at that time that they should pass their lives in close proximity.

They had now arrived at the epoch when the American Revolution had in reality begun, though not yet in its formal shape. It was not far from the close of this Revolution that Mr. Lowell changed his residence to Boston. This was evidently a wise step on his part. He had arrived at a very high standing in his profession, and was a leading practitioner at the bar in Massachusetts. The change was, no doubt, a painful one to the two friends. At that time the distance between Boston and Newburyport appeared very much greater than it now does. Then the journey from one town to the other usually occupied a whole day, whereas now it is ordinarily accomplished in two hours. The friends had passed through the great Revolution together, and had, I believe, agreed as to the principles which led to it. Of the two, Mr. Jackson was the more ardent and sanguine Later in life he was accustomed to say that, if it was so, it only showed that his "brother" was the more learned and wise, not more slack in promoting the great and glorious cause.*

Mr. Jackson was much engaged in mercantile business during the Revolution, but I believe that his thoughts were more occupied in the political concerns of the country than in matters of trade. Meanwhile his fortunes were various; when the war came to an end he had gathered around him nine children, the oldest born in March, 1773, the youngest in October, 1783. He had begun life with property derived from his father, not less than

* The family, who are descended from Mr. Lowell, have shown to their neighbors, in different parts of Massachusetts, talents so distinguished and virtues of so high a character that one is authorized to hope that their merits of every kind must always be known in New England.

20,000 guineas. This property was very much diminished in consequence of the war. Hitherto his prosperity had been comparatively very great. Now he felt that he was called upon for labor and industry and frugality. At this time he formed a partnership with Stephen Higginson, Esq., one of his most respected contemporaries. Jackson & Higginson engaged in commission business in Boston. To establish this new business Mr. J. left home in December, 1783, and visited Great Britain and Ireland, and afterwards France. In those countries he solicited consignments. At that time our whole country realized the want of foreign goods, but the supplies from the old countries were at very high prices, and in our exhausted state we were unable to pay for them. On his return home Mr. Jackson must have found the same embarrassments which existed in every part of the United States.

In May, 1785, Mr. J. removed his young family to Boston, that he might devote himself to his commercial occupations. In his new position his mind was filled with anxieties such as he held in common with all true patriots. Everywhere there was poverty and derangement of business, and the deepest anxiety, everywhere, regarding the establishment of law and order. We were ready to make laws, but the fear was whether those laws would be maintained and enforced. In 1786, when the insurrection occurred in Massachusetts, Mr. J. felt that it was his duty to take an active part for the maintenance of good government. He was one of the military corps who armed themselves as volunteers and went out to support public order. Shortly afterwards, when the gallant General Lincoln led a military force against the rebels, Mr. J. induced the General to receive him, as a volunteer, into his military family, there to render any service, for which he should be called upon, without looking for remuneration. The course adopted by General Lincoln very shortly met with success. At this period the General did his friend the honor to request him to take the despatches to Governor Bowdoin at Boston.

It was only in these temporary exposures that Mr. Jackson took any share in military transactions. In civil councils he was called out by his fellow-citizens or appointed by the Executive officers of the Government, and under these circumstances it does not appear that he ever failed to perform the duties which devolved upon him. Many years ago a story reached me from the Rev. Mr. Murray, a highly respected Presbyterian clergyman of Newburyport, to the effect that Mr. J. was engaged as a member of the Provincial Convention assembled at Watertown, where the members were occupied in warm debate. Their various suggestions having been offered as to the steps to be taken for the resistance to the British troops, it was said that Mr. J. then arose and proposed that they should at once dissolve their meeting, that each one should return to his own home and should carry to the army as many men as could be collected for the public defence. As there were no reports of public debates in those days, I have never been able to find evidence in support of this statement, nor has it ever appeared that Mr. J. made any attempt to lead his fellows in arms, but the writer feels assured that his father was never deficient in courage, and that it accorded with his character to engage in action rather than lose time in discussion. I presume, however, that nothing followed his proposal or led to any active steps.

In civil life, Mr. J., as has before been intimated, was not unfrequently occupied. How often this occurred I am unable to say. I will state only such services as I casually heard of and have kept in mind. During the hostilities between Great Britain and her Colonies the cities and towns became engaged, each for itself, in looking after its welfare and taking such temporary steps as from time to time were called for. In New England certain bodies of men were established as *committees of pub-*

lic safety. In this mode, though without any formal methods for organization, important questions were discussed, and measures adopted by which the public welfare was promoted and the public spirit advantageously maintained. In such committees it is very certain that Mr. J. frequently took a part in Newburyport. The Provincial Congress of Massachusetts was a body very analogous to these committees, although probably with more formality. In this, as well as in one or the other of the Houses of our General Court during the contest, or after that contest had ceased, he was at times engaged as a member; and near the close of the war, in the years 1781, and 1782, he was a member from his own State in the Congress of the United States. In the public engagements thus referred to, and as a private citizen, he always took part with those among the actors on the side of his country, who adopted the most liberal views, and among those also who were always ready to maintain good order. I will not omit to add that he always maintained the rights of those, whose political views differed from his own. He spoke with detestation of, personal ill-usage of his fellow-citizens who were deprived of their civil rights, or subjected to the seizure of their property, whether from injuries inflicted by the violence of a mob, or by formal steps such as were considered as legal or rightful.

Perhaps, in the foregoing notes, which were designed to be very brief, too much has been stated in detail. The writer, now near the end of a long life, was born during the great Revolution, so often referred to, and began to hear of that Revolution and of the measures to be adopted for the maintenance of government in the United States, before he could well understand the language in daily use on such subjects. What he has written depends upon the recollection of what he heard in his boyhood from time to time, from men he thought honest and well informed as to the current events of the period. Enough has been said in support of Mr. J.'s claims to patriotism and the love of good government. These notes are designed to accompany the portrait of the citizen, whose good name has never, I believe, been lost in the town where he spent the larger part of his active life, and where his children always felt proud to have been born. On his side, they have found his ancestors to have maintained the characters of honest men; and, let it not be omitted, that on their mother's side, they can trace their descent to an honest son of Ireland, who came from that country to the town of Newburyport. Entering its beautiful river as a young sailor, he there took up his abode for life. He sailed from there as a common seaman, and afterwards as a shipmaster. Lastly, he engaged in trade. In this occupation he was very successful, and maintained the character of an honorable merchant as long as his life continued.

In putting these notes on paper, the writer will take the liberty, in the name of his father's family, to express the great attachment they have maintained to their native town, and also to thank God for all the prosperity that has attended it, and for the high character it has always supported.

It should not be omitted, that within the last period of his life, during more than 20 years, Mr. J. performed various public services, not without much labor and great industry, from which he derived a support for his family. His labors, thus referred to, almost all consisted in in-door work for clerical purposes.

For many long days and many long evenings, with subordinate clerks about him, he was happy to obtain a support in his old age, and it was highly gratifying to him to find that the fidelity and correctness of his official services did not escape the satisfactory notice of the high officers in the Treasury

Department of the United States, under Washington, Adams, and Jefferson. A reference to the leading offices above referred to may now be added. The first of these was that of United States Marshal in the District of Massachusetts, then including Maine. The duties of this office were in general similar to those appertaining to that of the Sheriff's in our Commonwealth. Besides these there were two other services performed by him, which it will not be regarded as improper to put on record.

A few months after my father's appointment as Marshal, General Washington made a tour through the Eastern States. He began this tour from the city of New York, soon after the termination of the first session in Congress held under the new Constitution of the United States. This tour, which under a monarchical government might, perhaps, be called "a progress," was extended to the principal towns of New England. It was not, however, attended with such pomp and ceremony as I presume would have attended that of a royal personage. In the first part of this journey he was unattended by any official person. His private secretary attended him as such. As President Washington approached this Commonwealth, it appeared to the Marshal, or was suggested to him by some friend, that he should go out to meet the President and escort him while in this District as his constant attendant.

Washington accepted the proffered services very courteously, and assigned to Mr. J. a temporary place in his family. This honorable place he resigned on arriving at the borders of New Hampshire.*

There was another duty assigned to his office as Marshal by the Government of the United States, and one of much more importance, viz: that of taking the *Census of the District of Massachusetts*. This was the first census taken under the new Constitution of these States. The duty is required

---

* In preparing this article for the new Library, in Newburyport, I cannot omit to state, that in Newburyport as in other places, the town officers provided for the President a place for rest, &c. The house selected for this purpose was the very one in which the Public Library has recently been placed. On the occasion above referred to, it happened that Mr. J.'s family occupied, under a temporary arrangement, one-half of this building. In the other half, much of Mr. N. Tracy's furniture remained standing, and this was selected for the reception of the President. The introduction here took place in the evening, and Mr. Jackson then requested the honor of the President's company at tea. It had been well settled that the President would not make any private visits during this tour; and when Mr. Jackson offered to conduct him across the passage, Washington expressed some surprise, and seemed to feel as if he had been led into a private house by some undue influence. But the case was easily explained, and he crossed the passage with the same regard to etiquette which he always showed in small as well as in great things. The family well understood that this was not intended as an honor to them, but it was indeed a very high gratification to us children at least that they passed the night under the same roof with the " Father of his Country."

by that Constitution, and is a very important one; it is, as is well known, performed every tenth year. The first census was ordered in the year 1790, and called for great accuracy and fidelity.

Among the columns, under which were arranged the various descriptions of persons in respect to sex, age, or whatever else was thought proper, the last column was designed for the enumeration of slaves, as in the corresponding columns for each of the other of the thirteen States in our Union, and in the census of each of the other districts some slaves were reported. In Mr. Jackson's report of the Census of Massachusetts in 1790, he laid down the sheet on which it was written out, and I can never forget that on more than one occasion I saw him open the long roll, and on some occasions exhibit it to persons present, when he pointed out at the foot of the last column the written word, "*none.*" The *four* letters making up this word were, each of them, written in a round character, much more marked than in his common writing.

Before the Revolution, black slaves had been more or less frequent throughout the State, but as is well known, the maintenance of slavery had ceased about ten years previously. I may say that in Massachusetts the abolition had grown out of the high principles which belonged to our Commonwealth, without giving rise to any contest or to any ill feelings among our citizens.

With the exception of the official duties belonging to this new office, and those appertaining to the courts of law, the duties called for were, I believe, very few in the first two or three years after its establishment. The fees arising from this office were very small in amount, and to this fact Mr. Jackson probably drew the attention of the Government. He had not been seeking an appointment for the sake of the honorable distinctions to be derived from it, but for the emoluments of office, to which compensation it was thought that the sacrifices of time and money on his part during the Revolutionary War entitled him from the public. He now sought for some appointment which would be more lucrative, and this he obtained about the year 1791 or '92.

Among the duties called for in bringing the details of the new laws into operation, were those of collecting the *Internal Revenue* of the United States. The officers appointed in each district were Collectors, Inspectors, and a Supervisor.

It belonged to the Collectors to take the amount of the taxes due within certain limits appointed to their offices respectively. The Collectors thus appointed were required to collect and pay over the taxes to the Inspectors within whose limits they were placed. The same amounts when collected by the Inspectors were to be paid over to the Supervisor of each district, and appropriate reports to be made at stated periods. Finally, the reports of the Supervisor, and the duties collected by him, were to be made to an officer in the United States Treasury Department, called, if I remember rightly, the Comptroller of the United States Internal Revenue. Some other duties were attached to the office of Supervisor; but, in the District of Massachusetts at least, these were not of great importance.

In the District of Massachusetts there were three Inspectorships, — the first occupied the Counties of Suffolk and Middlesex, and perhaps all the other Counties on the South of Massachusetts proper. The second Inspectorship, as I believe, occupied all the Counties in Massachusetts proper not above referred to, viz.: Essex, Worcester, Hampshire, Berkshire, &c.

The third Inspectorship occupied the whole of Maine. It was of the Second District that Mr. Jackson was appointed the Inspector.

The head officer in the District of Massachusetts was the Supervisor of the Internal Revenue. When this branch of the United States Revenue was first established, the Hon. Nathaniel Gorham was appointed Supervisor in the District of Massachusetts. In the summer of the year 1796, Mr. Gorham died, and his office was left vacant. On this event, Mr. Jackson was appointed as Mr. Gorham's successor. Mr. J. accepted this office, and for that purpose he thought it essential that he should leave Newburyport, in order to have his residence in or near Boston. Finding himself obliged to take this step, he looked for a house in Boston, but not finding one there, he took one in Charlestown Square. There he remained from about the first of August. His children, from various causes, were dispersed about the world, and he thought it more expedient to go with my mother to some house in Boston where they should live temporarily as lodgers in some respectable family.

I was the only child at home with my parents. In the winter I had given up other business, and accepted a clerkship in my father's office for a year, residing in his family. Under these circumstances, he and my mother, in April, 1797, took lodgings in a private family at the South End, accompanied by a faithful domestic and friend, while I found a lodging near the office. The furniture we wanted was packed for removal, and everything in confusion, when, during the night of the 28th of April, my mother died suddenly of *apoplexy*. The change contemplated by her must have been not without some effect on her feelings, though none of us had been aware of it; she may have felt much in contemplating the change in her mode of living, although she maintained perfect composure in her appearance. Of course we were perfectly astonished and deranged by this event. We collected at once all the family within our reach. These were Charles, who had, the summer preceding, opened his office as a lawyer in Newburyport, and Patrick, who was then living as an apprentice with Wm. Bartlett, Esq., a merchant of the same town. My two older sisters were at lodgings in some pleasant residence in the country, and could not be easily called home: they were Hannah and Sally. The two younger of my sisters were at a boarding school at Hingham, so near to us that I drove down there and brought them home to attend the obsequies. On the third day from the period of her decease, my mother's remains were deposited in my father's family tomb, which now belongs to the estate of my brother Charles, in the Cemetery next to the Tremont Hotel, in the street now called Tremont Street.

About the last days of April, or the first days of May, 1797, my father entered on his new lodgings in Boston, and took me as his companion. Our landlord was an unfortunate young merchant who had just undergone his failure. He lived in a plain wooden house opposite to the grounds on which the Female Asylum now stands. The increasing misfortunes of our landlord soon caused him to break up his establishment, and we found new lodgings with a family in Federal Street. From early life my father had lived in large and convenient dwelling houses, and had for a long time been in the midst of a large family. It was impossible that he should not have felt this change from the life to which he had been accustomed, and the great loss of my mother could not fail to have a powerful effect on his feelings. With the firmness which belonged to his character he retained perfect composure. We lived at a distance from most of our friends in Boston, and he and I passed almost every leisure evening by ourselves. He was in his fifty-third year, I in my twentieth. Our conversation was without reserve. Without any formality in regard to it, he related to me from time to time the most minute as well as the most important and interesting events of his life. We became intimate friends, and, incidentally at least, he gave me many anecdotes of his acquaintances and friends at different stages of his life. Those of his statements committed to these pages were derived from these conversations, accompanied with very interesting details.

My father had then, and more or less through his whole previous life, many agreeable and valued friends of all ages. Among these he sometimes passed his evenings, and they not unfrequently accepted his invitations to dine. Thus his time did not lie heavily upon his hands.

A few months later, about the first of December of this year, 1797, I left my father, whose society had been so grateful to me, and began my studies under the direction of Doctor Holyoke, of Salem. My father remained in his lodgings in Federal Street, with his faithful guardian, Molly Knapp. His business was transacted in an office in a building still known, I believe, as Scollay's Buildings, in a large, comfortable room, having windows opening down Court Street and also on both the north and south sides of that building. From this time my own mind was devoted to the study of medicine, for the first two years in Salem. My third year was occupied by my passages to and from London, and my residence in that city. In this time my father's situation had altered much. His oldest daughter, Hannah, had been married to Francis C. Lowell, Esq., son of Judge Lowell, in the autumn of 1778, and his second daughter, Sarah, was married to John S. Gardner, Esq., a gentleman several years older than herself, who had never, I believe, been employed in any business for emolument, — an old bachelor physician had made him his heir, and Mr. G.'s mind had been engaged in liberal studies. He was supposed at the time to be rich, — and no doubt he thought himself so, but he had not learned how to employ his riches, and after two or three years he found, — what he had heard before, probably, but did not realize, — that riches were apt to take to themselves wings. He did not, so far as I know, incur any loss of property or financial embarrassments, nor did he appear to incur wasteful expenditures. He was naturally bright and lively in his deportment, and it was only by those who saw him familiarly that the waste of his means became evident. I who returned from my visit to London at the end of September, 1800, without any property, looked forward with sufficient confidence to gaining a support from professional labors, after having passed the usual period in preparation. I found that my father's emoluments from official labors were a comfortable maintenance for himself and his daughters. My other brothers were in prosperous circumstances, and were earning their own support, though no one of them could regard himself as rich. At that time it was manifest that my father was more bright in his feelings than when I left him. He was contented with the prospects before him, and that his ability to perform his official duties was not abating, but increasing. He had sustained a high and honorable character in periods of prosperity. He was retained in the office of Supervisor, more lucrative than that of Inspector, though he differed openly in his politics from Mr. Jefferson, while many of his friends in office were displaced. My father did not permit any apprehension of the loss of his office on account of his politics.

The sources of emolument to the Government of the United States were mostly those derived from the introduction of foreign goods. The taxes laid upon domestic products were small in amount. At that time the country could do well without these taxes. There was, however, an approval of the maintenance of these internal taxes. We were, of course, liable to unlooked-for expenses growing out of treatment of a hostile character from foreign nations. Within the few years through which we had passed since our new Government had been established, we had been brought into a state of hostility with Great Britain. Very shortly after the difficulties which then occurred had been removed, Great Britain was readily convinced that our Government neither designed, nor would permit, any departure from a due respect to her rights. She was at once convinced of the firmness of Washington in paying respect to her and to all other foreign nations, and perfect peace was established between us. On the other hand, the French Government seemed disposed to think that we were not willing to take up arms in her favor, and to become enemies to her opponents, and, ere long, they, as the English had done previously, seized upon our property on the high seas, and conducted towards us with even more violence than her neighbors had done. This experience, which I have stated very briefly, showed that our intercourse with other nations across the seas might at any time interrupt very greatly, if not entirely, the importation of foreign goods, and thus the collection of the revenue by duties on such goods might at any time be cut off.

It was easy to foresee, as it was foreseen by the most prudent and well-informed among our citizens, that instead of collecting an income from external sources alone, we ought to be familiarizing ourselves with the collection of internal taxes, and the sight of officers whose names were odious to us: I speak of tax-gatherers spread over the whole country, and requiring at every door the contributions requisite for the maintenance of our own government in peace or in war, and in the latter predicament, much larger supplies for the support of our armies and navies. Set aside these considerations, it is of no small consequence that the duties collected from foreign goods are not paid in each instance by the consumer. The articles furnished for sale are paid for by the merchants engaged in foreign trade. The tax is paid by the consumer as part of the price of the article imported. Although we all understand this, it does not seem wise to bring before the consumers at every moment the amount of taxes which is demanded.

The foregoing explanation may seem uncalled for, but I have made it because many of my readers may be those to whom the subject is not familiar. Let me explain then, that the financial business put into my father's hands by the Government did not fail him from any supposed deficiency on his part, but from the views of the Government, then lately established in power.

If I remember rightly, the change in the laws respecting the collection of taxes took place in 1802, or thereabout. Thus the labors in which my father had been engaged were brought to an end. Though his property had been increased a little in the last few years, he still found it necessary to seek for some profitable occupation. He was getting advanced in life, but his courage did not fail him, and he was happy to engage in such duties as he could perform with benefit to the community as well as to himself. Though not brought very much before the public, he had shown his ability as well as his readiness to undertake new offices, and he was not without some success. He was elected Treasurer of the Commonwealth of Massachusetts, and by successive re-elections he was retained as such through five years, this being the extreme limit to which the office could be continued.

During this period he also held for some years the office of Treasurer of Harvard College, and as such was a member of that corporation. Still later he was elected the first president of the Boston Bank; both the last-mentioned offices he held until the period of his decease in March, 1810.

So far as I knew, the performance of his duties in the various public offices in which he was engaged received the approval of those who were conversant with them, and in all cases were brought to a close in a manner honorable to him.

Let me now sum up some remarks upon my father's general appearance, and whatever I can recall which may help those who come after me in forming a just opinion of him. He was not a man who took a lead among those about him; at least not the first lead. He was not, however, one who could be passed over without observation in society. Most especially he felt and showed the greatest regard for the rights and feelings of others. Accordingly he was then just and kind. He not only paid his dues, if possible, but his heart always bore in mind the gratitude which did not rely on words alone. Kindness from others he could never forget.

He was given to hospitality. It was not only when he abounded, that he invited his acquaintances; but, when his feasts had become less sumptuous, he gave a welcome to his guests, trusting that a modest meal might bring with it a grateful relish. He made his services acceptable to his friends in whatever shape they were offered, and was distinguished by polished refinement of manners toward persons of all ages and classes.

It is necessary for me to bring these notes to an end. When I began, it was not without some risk that I might extend them too much, but I hope the subject will interest the reader.

It is now more than half a century since I lost my father. It would not be a singular thing if I exaggerated his virtues. From an early period of my life I not only estimated his character very highly, but I also loved him most deeply and most strongly. His justice and kindness to all men impressed me when I first became capable of reflection on moral excellence. I now recall vividly his love of truth, his fidelity toward his friends, and his reverence toward the Supreme Being, which led me to place him among the highest of the children of God, as one who sought to conform to the Divine laws, and to fulfil the duties ordained by the Great Teacher. Such were my convictions in regard to him, that, although I do not mean to represent him as faultless, I feel assured that his moral excellence has seldom been surpassed. By all who knew him he was regarded as an honest man and upright in all things, as well as kind and courteous in his manners.*

---

* Testimonials conforming to the eulogies stated in these pages, have come to me from various high sources, during his life, and since its termination.

Printed by Libri Plureos GmbH in Hamburg, Germany